LOST FAMILY

Lost Family

A MEMOIR

John Barton

THE POETRY IMPRINT AT VÉHICULE PRESS

Published with the generous assistance of The Canada Council for
the Arts and the Canada Book Fund of the Department of
Canadian Heritage.

SIGNAL EDITIONS EDITOR: CARMINE STARNINO

Cover design: David Drummond
Photo of the author by John Preston
Set in Filosofia and Minion by Simon Garamond
Printed by Marquis Book Printing Inc.

Dépôt légal, Library and Archives Canada and the
Bibliothèque national du Québec, third trimester 2020

LIBRARY AND ARCHIVES CANADA CATALOGUING IN PUBLICATION

Title: Lost family : a memoir / John Barton.
Names: Barton, John, 1957- author.
Description: Poems.
Identifiers: Canadiana (print) 20200281720 | Canadiana (ebook)
20200288601 | ISBN 9781550655551 (softcover) |
ISBN 9781550655599 (EPUB)
Subjects: LCSH: Barton, John, 1957-—Family—Poetry. | LCSH: Bar-
ton, John, 1957-—Childhood and youth— Poetry.
Classification: LCC PS8553.A78 L67 2020 | DDC C811/.54—dc23

Published by Véhicule Press, Montréal, Québec, Canada
www.vehiculepress.com

Distributed in Canada by LitDistCo
www.litdistco.ca

Distributed in the U.S. by Independent Publishers Group
www.ipgbook.com

Printed in Canada

for Pam, in memory

It struck me, right then, that some of us
on this planet are simply loved. That's all,
loved. The rest of us are umpires.
    —ETHAN MORDDEN, *How's Your Romance?*

CONTENTS

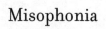

Misophonia

A Google Maps View
of the House Where I Grew Up

Why must I see it from above, the time
Lapse trapped in some undated spring I can't
Account for, the crabapples flaunting
Flesh-toned blossoms in the backyard climbing

Branch after retouched branch above unmown
Grass past the roof, ambition noted, beds
Impatient with daffodils dug up and spread
With added leaves below windows if blown

Up larger might appear undraped, emptied
Kitchen cupboards airless, footfalls scoring
Speckled tiles long stripped away, no present

Left to loiter through, petals shed, brainstem
Extant in unturned soil, the locked front door
Yellow still, impulse to knock hesitant.

Lost Self

Above and looking down before I was
Born, I saw myself looking back, the light
So strong it couldn't be seen through, a light
Striation of cumulus stretched across

Clipped lawn where I lay sprawled, each cloud shadow
A bruise capturing and losing its shape
Every pollen grain fixed under a scope
So sharp its lens was my eye, the meadow

Within starting to bloom as I pondered
Its insects and grasses, my body small
Observed from far off, my persistence all
The space between looking down and futures

Turned away, me knowing simply the self
Gazing upward, and to tenderness deaf.

A Twentieth-Century Roadmap
to Settler Architecture

The land was flat then, inarticulate

No trees stood against the sky, my shadow
The tallest structure I knew, two matched rows

Of houses the timespan of our street built

To affirm no opposites, drapes at dusk
Pulled across sightlines, childhood a crawlspace
The future rose out of, echoes sustained

By slide rules of dry air blueprints trusted
Open spaces drawing crossbeams of thought
Each roof the windblown wings of a city

New hypotheses, new towers ascending

Their assured axes the conduits I've sought
Through words, the freeways' clear tonalities

Blinding the stars with light past amending.

Campground, Canadian Rockies

The flashlight you call a torch picks our way

Along the lake, trunks of lodgepole it slides
Across are anchored in this spectral grey
Terrain we've brushed our teeth in, shade our guide

What your beam has kindled the footpath keeps

Slapping back, knuckles of poplar, needles
Elbowed from twigs, spiderwebs, dry pebbles
Of scat, sharp scent of kinnikinnick steeped
In sun, saskatoons bears could have eaten

And I start to sense what night sparks, hurried

From lat to tent, in sleeping bag worried
By what I can't touch (lonely stars bitten
From darkness by deep glacial water)

Scared by what I'll forget but can't alter.

Family Epidemic

I lie still. While you're watching us, they count.
Now calm, now still. Sunlight leads their fingers

Up arms they contrast, chicken pox mounting
By leaps both girls are eager to conjure

Motives for why it's jumped us so. Too sick
To care, I feel things itch where none is found

Sensing but not grasping why some are picked
To weigh early why we're void, small hands bound

In gloves you've cinched against my sides with gauze
To stop me scratching. Too raw for reason

Now calm, now still. My sister not pausing
Her inklings exponential, last to see

How we are marked piecemeal. You watch, patient
With our awe, my aunt, your witness ardent.

Fourth Birthday

The covered box sings in early sunshine
As I wake up, something inside jumping

From what might be a perch to flooring lined
With paper, a shade fingers must have crimped

Against my bedroom wall before I fell
Asleep, light left on to flicker after

Overnight turned melodic, the real's spell
Flapping behind a veil, rousing laughter

As I watch, head made clear, resting pillowed
In feathers before I rise to slip free

The drape on tiptoe from his cage, Peter
Never a mortal bird to deny me

His canary-yellow song, life's meter
Spondaic, lilt a flighty piccolo.

Nemesis of the Songbirds

In the a.m., on the AM station
You switch to, Petula Clark sings "Downtown"
And I freeze in mid-run through the kitchen.
How, in today's sunshine, can she feel down

But need to go shopping where glass buildings
Cast more dark than I guess, their cranes I'm sure
Are birds of paradise, wings spread riding
The whirlwinds they're prey to, up so high. Pure

Vista. Pure as her tone. How it bells through
Me, then is gone. Gone to ads about Coke
And Salada you never let steep, brewed
From pekoe dust, you fret, vexed I will mope

Doris Day switched off before she or I
Que sera, sera, can cheer up or cry.

Doing in the Dishes

Blue plaid: on the horizontal, pale blue
A blue black in vertical counterpoint

Day and night loomed through the cloud of this bowl
My favourite, every wind-tugged thread joined

To pull blue warp across a glazed concave
Whiteness where you let spill my cereal

At breakfast, a cradle for frosted flakes
Rocking in milk to make me jovial

Loopy with sugar, a sunshine habit
Turned turtle while learning to dry dishes

As you wash, your tall beside my little
The blue bowl sudsy till rinsed of wishes

And wiped with fact-finding care, indigo's
Vertigo flooring you when I let it go.

Misophonia

All through breakfast he makes his teacup chime
Plainspoken as a metronome, alarm
Forcing my back teeth to ache, spoon clenched
Between his index and thumb milling lumps

Of sugar through milk and taupey, mould-stained
Water, each cube a bathysphere I'm trapped
Inside, their hulls hammered by a tinkling
Maelstrom he slows, speeds up, cacophony

In freefall, patience stretched till I'm weightless—
Aquanaut awash among numb starfish
Saucer swamped, mopped up by the *Albertan*
Murky headlines fatal and tossed away

Before I've time to walk to school alone
Our street a calm uphill curve deaf to rhyme.

Momentary Psychopath

Age nine, I don't know why I chose her, girl
From up the street, shy like me, a twin
Me two-faced, a bully's tutored victim
Who one day stalked her, snuck up, and hurled

Her off her feet a block from school, the ice
We fell on gravel-sharp, her leotard
Ripping so I dragged them down, yanking hard
Waist below the knee when, shouts rendered hoarse

She fought with wiry strength and the cruel
Knowledge I stuffed her panties with, mud, slush
Melting down her thighs, not snow but a crushed
Dry ice blue as my glacial eyes, cold

Surprise when at last she began to cry
And I came to, let her go and the lies.

Nothing is What It Seams

The vein sewn in flesh-toned silk down the back
Of her thigh's not bleeding though it's torn
Clean through like her stocking. She could have sworn

She glanced both ways before she crossed; the truck's
Mirror, in slow reverse, caught no fragment

Of her slim legs, bumper bumping her off

Balance. A tap. A shock. Girl thrown to rough
Asphalt as nightfall spreads, no permanent
Bruising, but police are called. Her mink coat

Off the shoulder and moonlit. My father
Pulling her up as I gape in wonder

No outline of blood where she'd sprawled, endnote

To what I can't abstract from the body
As she's left to wait at a shop entry.

Homestead, Eastern Ontario

Searching for the churchyard where many lay
Amongst our mother's own, our father found
One alive and nearby, the sun rounding
Hills of scrubby remnant forest and the grey

Granite outcrops farmers had hoped to clear
And not wholly failed, a diorama
Against the sky's incumbent reds, grammars
Of long subsistence scripted in severe

Rainclouds slipping past while with directions
We drove for miles to a drafty brick house
Where a man who looked older than the coarse
Land he lived on, who with warm intentions

Recounted stories, fed and gave us beds—
I'd fall asleep unearthed, an arrowhead.

Malus Pumila

The paring knife you wield alertly flays
Paula Reds, Lobos, and Spartans alike

Skins loosed, their honeyed flesh quartered God-like
Before it browns, unprotected cores spayed

Practised strokes roseate, each shucked seed
Gravid womb in bits, tartly neatened to

Your plate's gold-flecked rim while you talk and chew
Distaste dispatched by etiquette's heedless

Untold rules while I, though well brought up, bite
Into my own still unnamed, freshly picked

Orbs, baby teeth ripping through wind-shined peel
Perched on the back step, cheeks churning cider

Till I swallow, onomatopoeic
Pips spat out so they may sprout in the real.

Postwar Philately

Bombardment, September 1940

"...flame came to be called 'a light,' they talked
of 'putting the light out'…"
—HENRY GREEN

Stunned, it hangs above the panicked city

Ailerons rimmed with fire, shorn fuselage
Igniting as it cartwheels, flinty edge
Of the nose wedging through a vacancy

Braced between facades on your narrow street
You angled from a tall window slit, large
Void above, the skies a spot-lit cortege

Somersaulting smoke corkscrewing from wings freed
To smash, on impact, the rapt blocks beyond
Russell Square after martyring the docks

An embered fall you wrote your mother of
Before signing up, nerve corresponding
To nothing you later flew, a flame caught

In ink and lit years on to spark my awe.

War Bride of the Atlantic

Sailing the wrong way, away from safety

It takes weeks to cross, the ocean a plane
Parting sky from seafloor, where U-boats feign
Sinking to, though below the phony

Mirror of harmless cloud, they wait, the lure
Of smooth seas camouflaging the hazards
Convoys zigzag over, meandering
To Bristol from Halifax, armatures

On alert while you keep typing reports
The captain dictates, sit at his table
Napkins creased as tersely as sails, able
For seconds to forget the three escorts

Torpedoed, made to stay awake all night
Should death's periscope really lift in sight.

From the Studio of Robert Fort

Victoria, November 11, 1942

They hung through my childhood in their bedroom
The Spartan frame armband-black, pedestalled
White mums on either side, her hands folded
His clasped behind his back, intent eyes calm

And uniform pressed, RAF issue
Her suit conscripted—she'd no time to buy
Or pin a dress, three days' notice—just shy
Of twenty, him older, wars to fly through

A mainland train to catch, their vows scripted
And mouthed back, her submission, his loyalty
Sleeping cars coupled with chagrin, or lust

Him the one good work she was not equipped
To best, her shock a gun with its safety
Jamming, though in their berth they aimed for trust.

Postwar Philately

> "It's not just the stamp that makes it valuable
> but often the cancellation mark."
>
> —NANCY KENNEDY, *Citrus Country Chronicle*

From orange jute bags of deposed monarchs
Flowers, fish, and pictorials of freed
Now kept aloof, mapped-as-pink colonies
I'd set aside dull portraits of forsook

Deutschland leaders scissored from the corners
Of brown envelopes, faces I'd not soak
Loose and hinge to my album, fear evoked
Without shots fired or voices raised, borders

Not crossed to plant a flag acclaiming why
Questions redacted before I'd ask them
My parents' timbre blotted out, losses

Poste restante, mailed across oceans live—
Behind each stamp licked glue of burnt human
Bones, saliva, blood, shit, rows of crosses.

Ardingly

On my bedroom floor, your oak tuckbox sits

Empty, sun pallid through leaves of varnish
Lifting off the sides and lid, astonished
Brackets of coarse wrought iron holding it

True, your padlock missing, but neither hinge
Tongues hanging loose from rigid clasps: the scorched

Air inside tart with steam and coal; an arched
Gate open to a platform where you cringed
Lining up for the school local; choked air

Breathed in, not long withheld to account for
The tightlipped boy cagey inside the man
You sang yourself into, in tune, barest

Quaver in your stutter a strangled roar
Nerves eased by the reserve this box sealed in.

An Immigrant's Guide to Formal Gardens

No wild prairie rose revives the boyhood
Farm in Surrey his father raised him on

Between terms at school, erratic boxwood
Detangling light across the tonsured lawns

Blooms, groomed for show in vases, vast as plates
The breeze deflowered, the bees as efficient

Gyred from stamen to pistil, buzzing straight
To cached hives, scattered larva opulent

Unlike the mummied root balls he unwraps
Rootlets dry as matted crotch hair, branches

Lopped close to the hip as each bush is trapped
In anemic earth, apprentice leaves blenched

In sun after months of nun-like slumber
The rosebuds he contemplates unnumbered.

Rhubarb: The Cold War Years

No sweetness, for him, was insufficient
—For her, being tart, tartness tantalized—
The bitter stalks she'd whack from her plants
Noxious leaves hacked off, each brutalized

Into buckshot as plosive as cough drops
Washed down with cornstarch, a powdering
Of clove, so each cough may stew with dolloped
Butter in crust, egg white a coda

Slicked on thin as blush, a cheek aimed at heat
Our family's hot face we'd watch her cut into
The point of his wedge bloody, rare as beef
Its bubbly skin he'd peel back, a gluey

Dewlap, spoon on sugar, a rainmaker
Hoping clouds show up, expecting thunder.

Kananaskis Country

Alberta Highway 40, August 1964

Why she chose to stay home I never knew
Pam in front instead, standby navigator
While I drew us maps, back seat my canoe
Dried fish and hardtack, paddle locating

White water in the Rockies in pursuit
Of La Vérendrye, a fur trade surveyed
Up passes through books I got wet, a route
I blacked in; the boy I was, left for dead

By rapids we'd run to find a campsite—
Without her, Dad unlike himself: stranger
Who made us laugh while frying us eggs, light
Flipping clouds over easy, forager

Picking berries no one else saw, gravel
And dust our car wheels raised without rival.

His Infidelity

A dinner rushed before the early show
With your lonely son, you would let me choose
Where we ate and what we saw, films unknown
To you, with actors you found uncouth, skewed

By ceasefire or guns, the transplanted heads
Of boys on sheep, nuclear sites broken
Into, angst's isotopes falling on dead
Conquered landscapes, any kind words spoken

Lacking weight or context, when all you'd sought
Was dancing, good manners, wit, or song, not
Pins pulled from grenades not yet thrown, the fonts
In the credits' finest print a skeleton

Key to what you'd ignored in scripts at home
Miles from Peck and Hepburn on set in Rome.

On the Armistice

You're dead. No one can make me wear
This poppy; plastic poppies in lapels
Deconsecrate desire. Stood in this square
Long shadowed by its stone memorial

I'm obliged by one minute's silence to mark
The day you mouthed marriage vows and planted
Seed for offspring in jagged ground, the stark
Pyrrhic victories of later couplings. I can't

Not forget. I can't not look. A mistake
As I solace the son I was, who looks
To how duty joined you, poppies staking
False claim upon us before the war took

You both, poppy casualties, pinned by fear
Arms laid down, taken up in postwar years.

Grief on Speed Dial

Sneaking outside his house, my sisters call
You minutes before he dies and twenty
Years since you and he last talked, your windfall
Of distance a blank slug, though certainty

Keeps re-minting your despair to stamp us
As yours, death flipping coins, with you wanting
To rest them, heads-up, on his eyes, love fierce
To the end if fast rubbed faceless, haunted

By what he thought you could live on, though soon
You'll outspend him, long after they pass me
The phone to hang up, leaving me alone

With your devalued sorrow and immune
To second-wife bribes, my love tendered free
To see him past where there is no dial tone.

For Our Father Who Sang In Limbo

Argument made you inarticulate
Stutter bested by her sharp, tone-deaf tongue
Your words flattened as they formed, the quiet
A silence she swept you into, your lungs

Pauses it took time to attenuate
The airless aspirations she clung to
Ebbing as you breathed them in, lost efforts
Little could annul even had you sung

Your ripostes note-perfect, not pitched askance
Yet, if once or twice she left you alone
You stood down your charged, misfiring weapon
What you aimed to say no longer advanced

In Allied camouflage: a smile unknown
To us played on tuneful lips you'd open.

To us, played on tuneful lips, you'd open
The words deadlock stoppered, if we could wait
Their cadence cautious still, but less lumpen
The urge to give them each a shape innate

What they'd made you like, a fly pulsating
Against a windowpane, on the wrong side
The trapped air you bumbled suffocating
And dry, cracks to glide through no draft implied

The boy your grandmother loved without pride
Before the choir she had you join offered
Solace, the vocal range it trained rising
In one's head, your speech hymnals deciphered

Timbre sliding from soprano to bass
Though forlorn still, as you aged, out of place.

Though forlorn still, as you aged, out of place
Displaced by war to the air, a pilot
From England drilled overseas, air base
Landlocked, spellbound checklist intricate

Above plain Alberta plains, your command
Of currents confident, the gusts rounding
Ably your aptly angled wing-flaps, grand
Vistas swept wide, air speed midair sounded

Out without halting, bearings reported
To the control tower as smooth and clear, sunrise
Chorused by the propellers' brisk purr, bled
Of night terrors, far from home, uncompromised

By Earth's tin ear, engine noises masking
Gravity's garbled chirr, brief but lasting.

Gravity's garbled chirr, brief but lasting
War cut short how you courted her, orders
Dispatching you by boat and train faster

Than you hoped, both awed by crossing borders
To ordinary wounds from love present
The continental divide its coda

Till, abruptly, west of graded ascents
Where ice melts into opposed watersheds
You detrained at Kamloops, no warning sent

Affirming your return, aloofness shed
To assert your pledge, shocked arrival more
Smooth-tongued than any words your own might rend

Her bouquet limp swifter than most foresaw
Trees stripped of falling leaves the wind outwore.

Trees stripped of falling leaves the wind outwore
My sisters, from airstrip's end, watching you
Take off, land; take off, land; the flights accrued
In Chipmunks and Otters winged you at war

Had ceasefire in Korea not re-scored
Peace's wanted, grounding fraud, air imbued
With caprices of fitful light you flew
Blindly into, outlook cold, open-jawed

As our family dog, grumbling in its sleep
Pointing to some felled bird, no landings steep

Before I was born despite the tensions
Between you and Mum, between east and west
No treaty signed but deterrence tested
In stalemate, your rogue affairs unmentioned.

In stalemate, your rogue affairs unmentioned
Until I came along you knew to keep
Your tongue still, nothing betrayed when you'd creep
Past my pregnant mother, truth jettisoned

No spluttered excuses tendered, passion
Spread *sotto voce*, though from your low-winged seed
I too you scattered, fruit love couldn't reap
On the lam once I'd dropped, resignation

Bared by your mistress in notes sent care of
Shell Oil Co., postmarked from Laguna Beach, Cal.
Composed among the orange groves and found

After your death in your desk, pink foxglove
In bloom, why you'd saved them sentimental
For years unread, how they wrote us profound.

For years unread, how they wrote us profound
The bars and notes, not the music, your life
Long hesitation would pace us, the strife
Within to find a voice—stammer wound

Tight the refrain we'd hear, guile's set list bound
To mute you more—you calm if coasting solo
Away from your wives and allowed to slow
The tempo, had you outlived them and sounded

A reprise, my sisters could have made soar
The parts they'd sung singly as girls, parrots
Rhyming off humdrum days to you before

You'd set right grade-school math, I, in concert
Carrying themes you'd let fly unexplored—
Argument made you inarticulate.

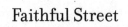

Faithful Street

Who, Where, Why, When

–Garry Neill Kennedy, *My Fourth Grade Class*
Lithograph on wove paper, 1972.

Trying his hand to write from memory
The names of anyone he's ever known
He annotates the photographs he owns
Or impressions he's made of them, every

One of them a shadow, light on paper
He's washed in aureoles of grey, shadows
Of shadows, the guessed-at names scrubbed of tone
Etched into the plate, powerless to escape

"Dick," or something less abrupt, scrawled as if
Tagged, tied to a baby toe, Lazarus
Loath to heed calls to rise, a forensics

Of last sightings as the wide-awake, stiff
Boys and girls they've stayed: smiling, embarrassed
the past's left them sitting still, still at risk.

Sleepover

The unfolded hide-a-bed we lie in

A floor below where my parents sleep calm
As effigies on light-worn, wind-scoured tombs

Holds us, pubescent boys unused to sin

Still pizza-faced, each stroking the other's
Unknown body, alike and unalike
The slick green wood we're cut from struck alive

By lightning we've trouble feeling, smothered

By skin no one's thus far lit, the scorched grain
Of our slow, half-kindled brains we reject
Even as we warm to what touch projects

To ease us past our opaque, birthmark-stained

Remorse, although we remain prehensile
And, afterward, back to back, immobile.

A Retrospective

Reconsidering the art of Christiane Pflug (1936–1972)
seen at a posthumous touring exhibition
at the Glenbow Museum, Calgary, April 1973

Her stilled lives moved me, her gaze as obsessed
As Kahlo's, though then I lacked any frame
Not my own to eyeball portraits of tamed
Dolls slumped in wicker chairs on successive

Porches, strict views of Toronto skyscapes
—Stock-still residential towers shadow
The DVP while commuters speed home
Aslant her sunless windows—no escape

Through drapes drawn open, no self-reflection
Ghosted in unapparent panes of glass
The face she'd left out felt as I walked past
Each work section by posthumous section

The first art I'd viewed, who I really was
Squared by each canvas, yet like her, absent.

Ars Suburbia

Clarity of the word, they always stressed
Parts of their speech, visceral my mother's
Tongue-tied pout, my father's tight-lipped stutter
Biting down on strict grammars of distress

The split-level where I grew up in black
And white, phonetic with alarm, front door
Slammed then tersely opened, my syntax scored
By a radio left on, the shellac

Finish chipped, speaker tinny, its voices
A jarring chorus our daft kitchen clock
Wanted to drown out or join, my bedroom

A soundstage for earworms I had no choice
In shoplifting earbuds for, air detoxed
By whispered lyrics, folk guitar my balm.

Pop Music Stigmata

First I tried gulping fifty vitamins
Capsules pellet-shaped, by gravity primed

To pop down my throat, hugging to the rhymed
Prospect of happy death I foresaw twinned

With existential, unthought-out practice
One-a-days repurposed to telescope

Into a placebo toxin I hope
Vaccinates doubt with courage, quick-acting

Not time-released as I lie down for real—
Absorption too slow to stop me thinking

Dosed and prone on this unmade dorm-room bed
Mouthing scratchy lyrics my hi-fi nails

Through me, needle skipping as I lip-synch
"Alive but that's the last thing on my mind."

Gefilte Fish

How to stuff it all in, the deboned carp
You poached and jellied with bits of carrot
And onion, spooned back into the intact
Skin you slipped it out of, glittery tarp

Of interleaved scales snug as a strapless
Formal; mouth zipped shut; eyes, chips of onyx—
What's plain fare for some, sharply exotic
To others, my plate picked clean, the hapless

Skeleton a ghost, the pool where it swam
Not fished out, silty savour of opal
Flesh fading on my tongue, what I recall

Of the clear broth you reduced for me crammed
With a strangeness not quenched without scruple
The trust you filled me with a swallowed jewel.

Trans-Linnaeus

Their name is Hydrangea, though in my youth
Hydrangeas flushed in manly blues no less
Showy than powder puffs hanging aloof
For all to see behind some truck's windscreen

Rear-view now sloped to reapply lipstick
A wetted fingertip arching once bushy
Brows in a pert-eyed compact, innate trick
Of how best to flower no longer abashed

Today's legerdemain hues from sapphire
To mauve, the chevron-shaped petals sans beard
Feeding on deprived intensifiers
For how to make a self, tipped into stirred

Wanting soils, a floral display unseen
In my boyhood, bloom I might have assumed.

Catalpa, Pansy

A tree too far north not to stand out here
Late to flower, unseasonable limbs
Winter-weary, searching, and cavalier
Voguing contrapposto beneath a scrim

Of leaves less see-through each time I stroll by
A fan dancer after a breeze picks up
Dusk rouging every heart-shaped leaf, a dye
Midnight sponges off, body paint usurped

Each morning once I'm awake and showered
Who I am long rushed down the drain, Ziggy
Starstruck stripped back to suits and ties for hours

Behind a desk, efficient, with a sprig
Of viola in my lapel, the bloom
Lion-faced and roaring all afternoon.

Faithful Street

Sun-Brite Laundromat
Cook Street Village, Victoria, 1980

Weathered sheets take me seaward: bedding shoaled
With shirts in my dryer's dime-spun vortex
As I walk past Faithful, rinsed by pale sparks
Chestnut lanterns drizzle, stairs a keyhole

Through foamy pink welters of rugosa
And broom the cliffs sheer off the foreshore with
Each tread down slippery, long-limbed kelp drifting
On stones the flow rumbles, lifts sub rosa

Waves advancing in abandoned washes
Of gritty, tingling, fast-withdrawing noise
Stirred-up sea glass unsound and jangling, poised
To be tamped against the sand, angles quashed

In the salt's pulse, beliefs pegged out to dry—
Until my cycle's over, I'm tongue-tied.

Ganymede's Coeval

The Romantics, Fall/Winter, 1980-81

Your eyes quiet each time you said my name
Our first conversations about Shelley
And Keats—coffee refills made us friendly
After class, tasked by term's end to stake claims

For "To a Skylark" and "To My Brothers"
—"Bird thou never wert," "a gentle empire
O'er fraternal souls"—both as exemplars
Of tones we'd begun sounding out, neither

Noting how resonances heard down low still
Could mark us, what we would rule out deeper
Than comradeship, pathos sensed but unplumbed

My desire to know you no less labile
Than my use of pronouns, grammars sweeping
Knowledge from forethought, doubtless to succumb.

Adjacent Apartments, View Street, Winter 1981

Knowledge from forethought, doubtless to succumb
Not awake to what a Kinsey 3 was
We fast fell in love with the same woman
A few months apart—the nineteen eighties

Barely three years old, unformed as we were
With longings starker than those now enjoyed
How we'd asked need to remake us absurd
Sudden self-belief opportune, not coy

Your bedroom across the building's courtyard
From mine when I'd woken you with a fist
Through my window, overhanging ivy

Bloodied, glass in my wrist—I took it hard
When she left: to love her a shattered risk
The moon deadpan, no contrition levied.

Shared Accommodation, West 15th and
South Granville, Spring 1984

The moon deadpan, no contrition levied
The empty, urbane nights I spent alone
While you studied: the stars, behind clouds, stones
Inured to what light they threw, not privy

To your thoughts as you left the library
The buses crossing False Creek to come home
Rooms we split unoccupied by hormones
The two of us celibate, and busy

I wrongly guessed, action I lacked supplied
Secondhand, the films I saw incessant
Their credits unreeled to prolong my stay

You disembarking to meet passersby
Men with dogs whose needs were urgent
Me not conscious of what I'd not betray.

Basement Suite, Gladstone Avenue, Fall 1986

Me not conscious of what I'd not betray
I came out through books I looked for or found
Falling into my hands, read below ground
With haste, not thumbing back or pulled away

Fictive worlds almost real, to be assayed—
From old suitcases I laid all I owned
On a raised, untried futon, caught spellbound
When one drunken night, I was met halfway

By your lips between unsealed, still creased sheets
Tongue spreading my legs bluntly indiscreet

Wanting to give everything I could take
Till drained but sated, withdrawing sticky
Adhering to plotlines you seldom faked
Fists thrust in pockets, gaze askance, nervy.

Athabasca Falls Room, Hotel MacDonald, Spring 1992

Fists thrust in pockets, gaze askance, nervy
As a plastic boutonnière, I toasted
Your bride ad lib, buttonholed by pithy
Gaffes in my wit, reflex boasting ghosted

By what, as rushed-in best man, I knew: roast
Not staged to be candid, guests hypnotized
As I extemporized about mileposts
On roads you took, stopping or racing by

The lie of the land not peopled or mapped—
A bootlegged scrim you posed her in front of
A photo cutout your heads poked through—tapped
As guide cum scene painter, I spoke of love

In ecofriendly terms: the vows to scale
Prospects viewed from dome cars not yet derailed.

1BR + Den, 12th & 12th, Summer 2002

Prospects viewed from dome cars not yet derailed
Her misgivings sharply raked, you struggled
To keep moving, the right of way upscaled
To dispel her apprehensions, trouble

A logjam you looked for groundbreaking routes
Around, the lawn dug up to loosen roots
Strangling the foundation, the outshone trees
As ungodlike as stray habits, raked leaves

Displaced by more leaves falling, purposeless
As remorse once you found yourself divorced
Wine we upended you hoped a trespass
We'd slyly embody, mine a clothes horse

Nothing more; re-dressed, I called a taxi—
How else to dial past being selfhood's proxy?

Return to Sender, Croft Street, Fall 2019

How else to dial past being selfhood's proxy
Or is it "truth" I mean—shaking cocktails
In Calgary, meeting your new fiancée
When I saw you last, how could I not fail

To rewind vistas you'd again drive through
The keys you gave her opening more locks
Than I could trust you to show her, foreknew
The detours you'd divert her to, the shocks

Responding to speedbumps she'd jolt over—
A dozen years later, I re-ponder
What I thought was clear, desire's quicksilver
Fugitive, love's bemusements enduring

Not knowing where you are, braked by your frame
Your eyes quiet each time you said my name.

Quo Vidas

Arrival and Departure

My collarbone lightly broken, you took

Me camping, marine layer damp in my hair
As I stepped off the ferry alone, bare
Headed, sunburned nose stung by kelp, and looked

Felt awkward till you stood out from the crowd
Waiting for foot traffic to clear Customs
Calm, sisterly, and pleased I'd crossed, the sum

Of the sea's pull, collapsed crash of surf loud
In my ears when years later I'm adrift

By your bed as two nurses unhook you
Your body a raft too wrecked to hold you
Here, unanchored as you seldom were, tipped

Safe, with provisions stowed and course plotted—
Our fingers' slipknot my grip can't keep taut.

In a West Coast Garden

Uncoiled wires of dove-grey hair the bristles
In her brush, with countless strokes, had pulled loose
She's letting fly, standing on her back stoop
A silver comb prizing them free with brisk

Swipes of a paring knife, jewelled scales parted
From filets of salmon with brutal strokes
Bones exposed and sloughed, flesh unshackled, soaked
In oil and lemon before poached with darts

Of thyme, her scalp showing through the fine cloud
Of her perm, a shampooed froth the wind drops
Through lilac and hummingbirds hoover up
For nests, one tensile, thumb-sized swirl shrouding

The small eggs her granddaughter finds and hides
A lock of her own hair kept should she die.

In Memory of Your Thirteenth Birthday

April 25, 1964

Why I got so wound up I can't recall
Re-see how Mum tried to wind me down, sent
Me to bed while you cut your cake, girl's scent
Of warm cherry franked on waxy smoke fouled

The air as I roared through my room, turned, slammed
My door on family stinks, talking silenced
Only dull mutterings of forks licensed
Against teeth as three mouths closed on the sham

We'd long called happy, bite by bite, rancour
The lasting gift I gave myself that day
Though you forgot it or just plum forgave
Your dark fruitcake brother and his crackpot

Knack for one-boy shows, how I could make you
Mad or laugh, scarecrow changed to cockatoo.

King Arthur in Hundred Acre Wood

For years after you should have left, you walked
Beneath the cover full-grown branches spread
Pages you'd leaf through mulched with shade, your bed
Made up in a forest hollow, Mum caught

At the oaks' lintel, how far she'd slip in
Milne had cleared a trusting path for, the bear
She saw etched over your shoulder squaring
With jelly paw-printed on the kitchen

Counter, her knives found stuck to the hilt
In clover honey, blunt Excaliburs
She drew out to make me wash, curt with lore
About absent-hearted boys, her pride spilt

In slights I'd lament, shelter found in woods
You would secret me into when you could.

Blessed Are

A double album cloaked in Christmas foil
Slipped among winter socks and books, hopeless
Untried vinyl to stack and observe drop
The discs played, removed, flipped, restacked, the full

Unscratched vibrato of her voice well travelled
As the platter on my portable turned
The stylus grinding Dixie down, the stern
Resistance of the frets she pressed, civil

Protest string by string touch affirmed: your gift
Pathos grooved in ethos; an acoustic
Spinning, a revolution spun inward

Sister tuning brother, Baez a lift
From self-doubt, notes of witness ecstatic
The spindle's gyre upending all I'd heard.

Butterflies Are Free

With chevrons of suede joined by crochet
To make an outer you halve, line, and stitch
Up two sides, the shoulder strap tacked on, rich
Umber and tan diamonds an interplay

Of tinny folk songs and soft-focus lights
Lost era of macramé, of sand candles
New purse a harlequin's belled cap dandled
Down your back behind moonlit hair, cold nights

Walking home from class, from experiments
Made to bloom under grow lamps in some lab
Any maturing you've aimed to replicate

Not felt as your own, youth re-invented
For flawed times, its style not then viewed as drab
A bag you give away, game to pupate.

Between Bullet Trains

This hours-long stop's name you know, see yourself
Holding a pen to surely transfer it
To a sealed envelope, your cursive crisp
And probing—lightly inked, unclouded proof

You'd let notepaper unfold to a girl
From this town, warming her to faraway
Mountain peaks you'd watch go icy blue-grey
From your bedroom window, foothills' snow whirled

To Japan, melted since—and you wait here
In middle age, unused time on your hands
Between trains, so you look for and find her

A cloudless voice she'd let fade again heard
Her albums browsed till, there you are—hair blonde
Brushed the same as now, eyes at sixteen clear.

Call From the Top

The tree is up and presents all present
At its base as foil-wrapped blocks of ice crammed
Close while at my stove, Mum boils, her current
Agitation stirring me in, the ham

And scalloped potatoes not yet cooking
Tardy foretaste of what goodwill I've lost
Cajoling me to juggle flatware, look
For apter settings when you call from the top

Of the world, only Everest higher
Where you are, cloudless phone line above Katmandu
Warm with chill; long distance not leaving you
Disembodied, your face all voice: sapphire

Moonlight bounced off snow millennia thick—
Your presence clear, melting me to the quick.

Late Show, Minneapolis, 1977

I dragged you to *Outrageous*, but could not
Tell you why as the faux-deco movie
House was nimbly lit by the outré plot
Robin flipping from Liza to Judy

From Marlene to Barbra, every diva
He urged on stage with a turn of his head
Shrug of his shoulders, hips cantilevered
From beneath sequins, nonstop arms outspread

Their voices his for a New York debut—
You not asking much before the credits
Surged past, borne on the wake of his rubies
Who I was: rhinestone loose in the setting

Of a paste solitaire, marquee still on
As we drove off, car cold till we got in.

Sister, First Landscape, Climate Change

Sundays, often, no matter the weather
We'd load the car and drive, the mauves we sought
Turned rock-solid by the sun, a lather

Of snowmelt rinsing, dazzled crags, Dad not
Averse to backroads, apt to veer off track
Mum, aware he'd not swerve us straight, distraught

The trails to scale on her map might be packed
Too thin the dry air she pined for, the two
Of us with windows rolled down, what we passed

Trapped behind them breathed in, the changeless view
As foothills became mountains, always sheer
The abrupt slopes we watched ascend, raw blues

I took to heart, climbs death would later clear
For you, for them, mine to orienteer.

For you, for them, mine to orienteer—
Never had I guessed it would come to this
Though, sent to camp once, alone I appeared

To disappear, nothing truly blissful
About solitude among other boys
On the shores of Lac des Arcs, an abyss

The dam at Seebe held back to annoy
Undercurrents pinned by Mt. Yamnuska's
Shadow, against whose wall of stone each ploy

To make me rock-climb left me hanging, trust
Tangled up in an unplumbed lack of depth
Perception, just how high to scale a risk

I couldn't eyeball, the drop down a myth—
Bottomless the freefalling strain of growth.

Bottomless the freefalling strain of growth
With too little guidance or far too much
We'd walk along the ice-fed creek frothing

Through Johnston Canyon, never losing touch
With what made us walk, you and I, the drive
To swim in the Ink Pots at trail's end, rich

With dye, jade water soothing us, deprived
Of long showers, but exhilarated
Retrospect a viewpoint to be revived

Its reward the hot springs we'd ideate
On the walk out, a shared, relied-on heat
In our bones already, aches frustrated

By motion, not by hope turned obsolete
By its fulfillment, water steaming, deep.

By its fulfillment, water steaming, deep
Aspiration overworks the landscape
Primed to inspire it, surveyed mountain peaks

Lasting but arid, our persistence scraped
From their clear-cut flanks, a failing climate
Effacing the glaciers, cirques agape

Naked layers of rock none can interpret
Without regret, so reimagining
The Bow River's gouged floodplain, I admit

I had wrongly supposed we could, within
Limits, walk existing banks, curves and course
Set in stone, current swirled through treed margins

Only to leave me to hike to the source
Alone, flow mutable, my lone voice hoarse.

Alone, flow mutable, my lone voice hoarse
In echo of how they spoke, case in point
The silent path Dad beat about Mum's force

No show of strength could erode, no affront
She'd brook he withstood, circuitousness
The one way to meander past the brunt

Of her *genius loci*: lightning professed
To cleanse the air before dull thunder rolled
The aftereffects of love I'd not guessed

Would later shape how we'd unscroll
Our longings, the near-vertical tumble
Of spring thaw chilling while snow lasted, sole

Route down from peak to valley fumbled
Scree thrown in our way to make us stumble.

Scree thrown in our way to make us stumble
It drove us to scatter, runaway shards
Skidding past us over drops to jumbled

Slag of a once-sequential, deluge-scarred
Geologic record, our family
Tree anchoring between laid-bare, ill-starred

Unstable layers, invasive species keyed
To spread wide its branches, the lofty crown
Out of balance with the root ball, degrees

Of transience cruel to fathom, bound
To let us go, our older sister gone
Years before we had grown, down

Side up, our straying roots exposed and stunned
Against vistas we had to move beyond.

Against vistas we had to move beyond
I compare all other landscapes, measure
Of how I've acclimatized and respond

Cliffs I walk along not reassuring—
Peaks casting a close-to-snowless presence
From across the strait, sun-battered and stern

Avatars of where we started, immense
But distant: our time together, though felt
As endless, short-lived: slopes in the end rinsed

Of any trail we'd made, remnant snowmelt
Washing it away, runoff labouring
To sea, the higher tides lifting the fault

Lines of surviving debris to cold air
Sundays, often, no matter the weather.

Quo Vidas

Last time I saw you, you'd lain dead an hour
Life support switched off and the tubes removed
Figure inert under straightened layers
Of fleece and cotton, askew knees louvered

Closed below chest, bowed arms anchoring breasts
Hair forced back from a high family forehead
Not how you might have fixed it, face eclipsed
Unmasked of blush, lips and eyelids shut, bed

Cranked up behind pillows your shoulders claimed
Sighing backwards. The last time I saw you
Alive, we split the long-drawn-out remains
Of lunch, the deli's steel awning corkscrewed

Open by your laughter, husband observed
Quaffing the Prosecco's dregs, unconcerned.

Tchaikovsky, Age 52, Finds His Inspiration

St. Petersburg, Paris, and New York, 1892

Their antics awkward, he consents to score
Mouse soldiers, candies flouncing, ropes of hoar
Frost enthralling forests of pine, a nut
Cracker too tight-lipped to voice the stunted

Prince within, the entr'acte lacklustre
Lead orbs drooping off the bough, sputtering
Candles shunning flame, few snowflakes waltzing
Some cloying waif named Marie or Clara

Too slow-limbed to pirouette or soar
Till flu fells his sister, her vanished pulse
Restringing blown snow, crystallizing cor

Anglais, celesta, timpani, and harp
The witless whittled prince unshelled a man
Making steps for her, no horn abandoned.

Keepsake

A small burnished square of Taxco silver
You'd intuited my finger could slip
Through without it slipping off, the hole's grip
Above the knuckle made for spin, shivers

Of light played across the hammered facets
I'd glance at and reflect on while we'd talk
Our banter wrought from the not-recast torque
Of turns and twists life wrung from us, tacit

Hold of what we'd need respite from, recalled
Ways of laying tables, napkin rings, towels
For guests, politeness not deemed as awkward

Habits of address set even if scrawled
In letters or sent by email, love held
By mirrors we silvered, could never blur.

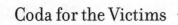
Coda for the Victims

My Ackerley, Myself

You were the most genial man he'd met
Forster said, a new friend decades older
Your height and spartan gaze making you bold
A one-time prisoner of war who kept

Shirt-lifting guardsmen in the damp shadows
Near Marble Arch, your wash-and-wear candour
Ill-fitting payment, unlike the stature
Of your poetry, the cleanness of your prose

You always came too early, excitement
Or fear, no anodyne man satisfied
Gratification, disrobed, not the point

A dog why you walked on the Embankment
In your abstinent last years, wrote its life
Which I've read and cannot forget, or won't.

The Loneliness of Everett Klippert

A mechanic admitting to certain
Carnal acts with those males who'd sought repair
He found himself with no jack in prison
Three years times four men, injustice tarring

Him a dangerous intimate offender
To keep his hands and mouth away from tools
Ones of unlike gauge at least, however
Well, if asked, he'd oil them, despite the rules

Decades ago—his release engineered
After piled-up, junkyard years no one'd held
Him, warehoused him in a cell barred by fears
Nothing could corrode before it's unsealed

And he's freed, dies guiltless but unpardoned—
Forfeit's engine not flushed out for thousands.

Giovanni's Room

> "I am too various to be trusted."
> —JAMES BALDWIN

Bookstores took its name in many cities
And pubs in others, as did side-street clubs
Where men sent drinks to men, sought sex, found drugs
Some in dark backrooms since the pitiless

Shelters it limns defined—the cold, off-track
Sanctums scorn found to avoid itself in
Walls and bulb naked, undraped windows dim
As those self-hate waxed to hide the airshaft—

What we paged our lost way through, the squalor
His words blew open, a door to sunlight
And cafés near the Seine, to the matchless

Rive droite, Haussmann's thoroughfares claimed as ours
Outside the law: Baldwin, cigarette lit
Drafting from guillotined shame a chrysalis.

Bathhouse Raids, Toronto, February 1981

"Reality is fiction, writing is truth:
such is the ruse of language."
—ROLAND BARTHES

That they may have stood outside in towels
Resists analysis since I don't know
If police lined them up down Yonge, exposed
To cold and cameras, names taken, allowed

No cover after couples were decoupled
Embraces split and tongues withdrawn or worse—
Men cuffed with slurs lust can't mouth, perverse
Unease ad hoc, rubbed dry without scruple

But to make words come clean, to leave behind
Remorse, let me say named and unnamed men
Later gathered clothed in anger, men caught
No more, but candid agents undefined

By all agencies not their own, the streets
Frank, stripped down to laws discreet not discrete.

They Always Get Their Man

Bruce Weber, *Extras at Zoetrope Studios*, Los Angeles
Black-and-white photograph, 1985.

A well-rehearsed repertoire of stances
Turns them face to face, grins unassuming
Bill's red RCMP tunic undone
Brass buttons flashy, bare chest a costume

He has long longed to wear, Paul's eyes giving
Him definition, rib by rib, a wide-brimmed
Campaign hat cupping Bill's crotch, the crown stiff
Grazing a sunburnt thigh, the toughened skin

At ease, easy on the eyes, Paul in matching
Regulation pants, 5BX-trained arms
And shoulders shirtless, scapulae sweat-lubed

Back's trapezoid torqued above a turning
Waist where Bill's yet to lay his hands, disarmed
Poised to tease his belt through Paul's untried loops.

The Love Song of Dusty Springfield

"At night the people come and go
They talk too fast and walk too slow."
—PET SHOP BOYS

Born as Mary Isobel Catherine
Bernadette O'Brien, I've let myself drown
In the swamps of sloe-eyed soul, its tailspin
Spun through muddy octaves the blues unwound

Across barbwire staves, my torn notes sultry
Countless hit singles about loss turning
On itself, an ouroboros hungry
For calm, a diamond needle burning

Stasis in circles through vinyl, nosedive
Voice a rose window, my jaw broken
By the woman I still love, my beehive
The ache I keep sprayed in place to strengthen

Unheard prayers climbing scales blown off course
By the heartbreak I sing hurricane-force.

Twilight of English Pastoral Art

The rambling lower boughs entangle light
In washes the rain-dry cedars filter
Skyward down, green-needled perimeter
Undercut with camouflaging browns night

Turns crepuscular, then Wordsworthian
Traces cut through old growth meandering
Friendless as the men who blaze them, laundered
Trousers unbuttoned and breast pockets torn

Paint rubbed thin under the finger-soft tread
Of boots shushed by leaves repeating circuits
Incised through laid paper's receptive field

Lust's underbrush of love artless, woods bled
Of cross-hatched paths no limb-barred moon admits
What's not sunlit unabashed, risk annealed.

Rock Hudson, Safer Sex,
and What Comes Next

I watch as his chartered jet is shadowed
From Paris to LAX, no time left
Except to fly home and die, fans bereft
What's taken many has claimed one they know

Their matinee idol a worn-down face
Re-sculpted by Kaposi's sarcoma
What's chiselled him makes sick my prime, comas
Of unease woken to and from, displaced

Denial not displacing my desire
Fear, stripped back to, slaked by coming on strong
With caution, coming often, pariah
Libido constrained and contained by long

Hours I unroll on my lover's cock, thrusts
We keep under wraps to seal in our trust.

School of Xerez Fino

for J-F, January 1987

Toxic, the club where we met, rundown now
Rundown then, the johns sequined with beer, dim
Crush of moon-flesh dancing, the strobe's freeze-frame

History painting a stock animation

Mirror balls, matches, condoms, sweat-raw limbs
Shedding shirts, shedding disco; shrill amyl
Nitrate; Doc Martens; plucked or pierced eyebrows
Ripped chinos zigzagging tans; shyness shunned

Sherry your cheeky decanted ploy to haul
Me home to fortify us both, pouring
Dryly from our clothes after scorching cold
Flamed our skin, run-from din making you bold
Air smokeless, one candle lit, till you wore

Me out and down, our legs dawn-slaked and sprawled.

After Rereading *Eighty-Sixed*

> "They'll take out a contract on me and write eighty-six:
> Terminate with extreme prejudice."
> —DAVID B. FEINBERG, 1989

Was public health ever useful to guys
We had met on the street as zipless fucks
Interchangeable physiques coldly shucked
Of Lacoste T's and 501s, capsized

In waterbeds to sink past need, excised
As "been-there-now-who's next" from address books
Consciously revisionist before tucked
In pockets against hardened glutes, revised

While we sat by hospital beds, fluids
We'd swapped contact also had corrupted

Unsought exposure naming us and them
Random men we had barely known laid bare
As dying friends, a helplessness to bear—
Only when recalled do we live, *pro tem.*

For David Wojnarowicz

Born 1954, died 1992

His father beat the suburbs out of him
Before he ran away and he began
To seek stills within, a wide-angled lens
The country he'd screwed his way across, slim

And ruthless, tender in f-stops to come
His New York no one wanted to rebuild
Where he could sell himself, shoot drugs, feral
On Avenue A till he watched too young

Too many men die young, film spooled to see
Them waste, his eye a window forced open
On whitewashed walls, the concealed air vents real

Not pre-invented, men lost, and those he
Shot unedited, his hand-held weapon
Fatal: love bleak, lacking outtakes, not zeal.

Age of Foolish Risk

How could I have known I had entered you
Under false pretenses till some local
Weekly I picked up after focused
My fear of illness, stated you had sued

GMHC for unjust dismissal
The through line extending as ironic
Probable cause your luckless status, sick
And unthinking, my sense of self annulled

Twenty mute years later finding myself
Keen to confess I was aroused and stupid
Should have asked you, not played empty-headed
Stayed on top in ways more than one, you a wolf

Not to tell me, hinting it was my choice
Not to wear a condom and lose my voice.

Love's Twin

My radio switched off, I walked to work
U.S. embassy without barriers
Peace Tower's morning shadow a flame carried
Forward by leaves pulled through the canal's mirk

Becalmed current mirror-still, the quartz air
Bright with a chill I felt with relief, stung
You wouldn't visit me, what we'd shared hung
In suspense, your rancour about to flare

The first plane a starburst through the North tower
Before I reached my desk, the second's heat
A sword winged through the South before your hate
Felled me when you called, love's exploding star

Burning my hands, phone incinerated
Worlds collapsing, the personal prostrate.

Folded On the Steps of the Museum
of Broken Relationships

What numbness you've left me no detergent
Will lift from fabrics it's worked itself into
A regret so true the weave can't loosen
To let pass, my flesh coarse, naked when dressed

The shirts I gave you kept in my closet
Washed, or new and unworn, no other man
As slight, shoulders trim, upholding the span
Of yokes stitched and re-stitched till they would fit

The stranger in you, buttoned and polished
My off-the-rack tears and sweat binding them
To your skin, unknowable to both of us

Who you are: a shirt no iron could touch
Lassitude you let slip off without blame
Light dropped to the floor as your shape was lost.

Life Drawing

To lay down one line and find a likeness
The body caught in a single gesture
Expression in the touch, the skin-toned chalk
Held loosely, lightly, the slightest pressure

Leant into: from the shoulder, a movement
Through elbow, wrist, to fingers, paper looked
Away from, not at; flesh as thought; dormant
Knowing called forth not trespassed (chance mistook

For fate; fate for chance) as what's found is joined
By more lines, body static in time-lapse
What the skin hides implied, not purloined
But worked out; each drawing a capsule

Forgotten until lifted from the vault
What's seen in it, when laid flat, not faultless.

What We Live For

We stop for one night, our last bed cradled
By cloverleafs and strip malls, the theme parks

Closed, the missed magic we'd sought cooling, marked
By swampy vistas, lust lacking credo

Where desire's falling flat and stays so, greens
And reedy, blood-warm, slow-flowing aquas

Lacking depth as we spoke less, insect buzz
Outgunned by engine revs as we drove, keen

To sleep, wake, then fly silent and away
But hours after shootings in Orlando

You dream, out of reach but safe, while I hold
A candle, recall Latino men slain

Dancing at a gay club where we once would
Hate like love abrupt, unnoticed, not dead.

Coda for the Victims

It takes no self-consciousness to guess how
A landscaper could pick them, the tapped swipe

Of their profiles, such null bodies his type
Disassembled already by the cropped

Gaze of their smart phones, parts isolated
From their eyes, shaved or engorged, trunks of brown

Skin oceans away from home or ground down
By what being born here has made them prey

To, invasive species he would text lines
And root from cover with the funk of sex

Horny men used to rough white hands not death
Stripped limbs he disjoints before he consigns

Them to mulch he rakes flat, unseen index
Of those too few miss, us all psychopaths.

The London Patient

"Such great news for so many."
–DONALD J. TRUMP, March 5, 2019

HIV near felled him, yet he's not dead
Antiretrovirals defending him
The life he's returned to long leaving him
Prey to cancers he had not expected

To be undone by, death again in play
The drug cocktail tipping him from victim
To survivor upended, future dimmed
Undetectable while he's plainly flayed

By illness before transplanted stem cells
Not unlike the Trojans he once rolled on
Stem his tumours, the arrested menace

To his T-cells not now a peril quelled
But gone, viral the news eureka spawns
As without firewall it spreads, contagious.

HIV: A History

We were undetectable till the bug
Recast desire as threat, a death sentence
Attraction couldn't commute kiss by kiss
Those noticing us get sick hateful, smug

Not guessing the virus eschewed constraint
Copied body to body, blood tainted
Despite how or whose genitals were joined
Time foreshortened and illness unchecked, coin

Upon coin laid on eyelids till our rage
Rewired response and undetectable
Rewrote itself as untransmittable
Drugs luring seroconversion offstage

Contact between contacts without buffer
The risks from love making fewer suffer.

Larry Kramer

"We must love one another or die."
—W. H. AUDEN

Immune to how illness claimed its patients
Indifference could not fail to command
His blunt critique, infectious impatience
Broadly short, tone jaundiced with reprimand

Hyperbole a side-effect alleged
More exponential than the deaths he feared
A prognosis demeaned by those who hedged
His advocacy hoarse, stats in stopped ears

A voice all he had, taunting ignorance
Without pause, an unapologetic
Incivility he gave legs, advanced
Along Wall Street, placarding pandemic

Spread to arouse the incautious living
His scorn prophylactic, unforgiving.

Kenny's Bracelet

A twined, hammered twist of what's left of him—
Nickel, copper, brass: a glinting soldered
Echo you heard, found as his apartment
Was emptied out, noise-tamped studio dim

With what became the East Village, retro
When gentrified, how he lived forgotten
What killed him a virus loving thousands
Of men, an artifact, the past's scarecrow

Outstaring fear, garbage cleared from Broadway
The ignored way he died not how we are
Let go, dying now, his bracelet a scar
You wrap about my wrist, longing reclaimed

A molten link my skin warms, how like me
He used to sit, hands clasped about one knee.

Melittology

My Mother, Unconscious

While she coasted, I pulled a chair beside

Her bed, restarted browsing Isherwood
A memoir of Kathleen and Frank I should
Have kept with years ago, not put aside

My willful abandonment a coma

Not all sons yield to, our parents long dead
To us before they die, love underfed
No solace offered, eyes turned from trauma's

Kill site, till at last death issues notice

And, summoned, I dig trenches as Frank goes
Missing at Ypres, a loss care imposed
A father his son locates through practice

Of renewal, letters read, pictures drawn
My mother close, lightened as his lives on.

Wasp, Queen

Minneapolis, August 1970

Up it flew while swords of gladioli
She chose dropped, a mauve slaughter at her feet
Bell of her dress flaring, amplifying
Her flair for improv, hem swept high to free

What zigzagged her stocking, a tripped running
Muddle of girdle clasps and tap-dance hops
Under the flower stall's canvas arch, stung
Lurch to a lamppost where, right on the spot

She rolled down her nylon-top, kicking off
A closed-toe shoe—less Liza Minelli
Than Jean Harlow, vampish, with her midriff
Exposed, or barely—such swagger nervy

And over in seconds as, awed, we watched
From the car, my mother seldom so caught.

Melittology

The swelling down, the doctor said no sting
If one this paltry hadn't killed me, could
My sensitivity misunderstood
As always, despite my taste for walking

In shorts through tall breezy fescues waning
At the city's underfed margins, woods
Hectored by wasps and free-wheeling bees, good
Boots and argyle socks not enough to bring

Surprise to heel, the first grassy stumble
I recall making me, a child, humble

The hankie Mum knotted about my thigh
A tourniquet cinched tight to stem the pain's
Righteous spread: when undone, what drew my eye
Were violets the stinger stitched through muslin.

A Son's Nineteen-Seventies Wardrobe

"What the hand, dare seize the fire?"
—WILLIAM BLAKE

Consider a new habit—classical
The skill she used to embroider my new
Jean jacket with roses, new leaves sprinkled
With runoff-blue, stitch-sized raindrops I knew

She took pains to make look real, knew she strew
Down vines buds yet to open, newly dropped
Petals around our patio renewed
In floss about the yoke, new deadheads lopped

But unrecorded, my youth a new crop
Of years she saw I'd not share, new threads
She bought me made newer still, sprays cupping
Shoulder blades newly squared, a blind spreading

Across my back, a newness I'd not see
When worn, nor the tiger she knew I'd free.

How Too Late I Came To Understand You

You contested every step across the Thames
Westminster Bridge not long enough to turn
The argument away from streets I'd learn
Should I walk them each night to Soho, men

You'd never talk to taking me to bed
AIDS-starved shades no lonely parent can shield
Her son from (prophylaxis revealing
A faith in my appeal I'd not best), then

Gave up, let me slip down Shaftesbury Road
(I drank bitter, slunk back to our hotel)
Four sober London nights with infidels
Flipped for one week in Scotland (foreboding

Swapped for calm), a room with twin beds we shared
Both sitting up to read, coats hung from chairs.

Camus' *Outsider* from the Inside Out

Today his mother died, or so I've read
His articulate initial sentence
Open in my lap years after I closed
It first, words I keep rereading, fluent

In how no mistranslation can change
Harsh clarities in the prose, the sun
In Algiers bleaching out whatever range
In tone he had known, a man undone

The rogue unknowingness of who I am
Holding the pistol as if I had fired
The unreadability of blocked aims
Gaps in insight forensic, if desired

The void I felt before my mother died—
No ellipsis numbly lived wholly lies.

Scrabbled

A logos of letters spelling the end
—*Nemesis, omega, finis,* or *death*—
A few of us game to lay words to rest
Cosmic orthography portended

By this wonky Ouija, fate stared down
Plugged into the acrostic we're making
A found poem of found poems, meaning at stake
Suffixed or prefixed, import less grounded

Tile by tile as s*ense* becomes *nonsense*
Not *sensei, chi* leads to s*chist* or *chime*
Until there's nothing left but *i, i, i*
Dementia's detritus outlasting context

The players either aphasic or bored
The letters all gone, blanks without stories.

My Mother's Anorak

An unwarned-of downpour makes me grab it
From my closet and put it on, my arms
Shoulder-deep in her sleeves and I'm disarmed
Although the zipper keeps jamming, it fits

My body replaced by hers as she steals
Fresh air, a disenchanted imprinting
Glare blazing from my eyes, her damning squint
I've not for the first time felt within, steel

Muffled will too snug before I have shrugged
It off, red waterproofed temperament crumpled
Which, when alive, she'd turn to the weather

A drear caution would make me forecast, tugged
At storm by storm, her eyes salt, blasts levelled
To stagger me with blows love gusts farther.

Love

I watch you eat, humble but diligent
The way you'd shown us, as children, to hold
Knives and forks, paper napkin unfolded
Between crumbs and lap, neither elbow bent

On the table, unforgiving posture
A cliff, as yours now is not, curled over
An emptied plate, checklist of manners
Plainly as robotic as the fractured

Destiny we meticulously share
Your bearing toward me, since birth, unclear

Till, spooning through today's bowl of peaches
You blurt "I need you" with such deadly force
I'm awed, obligation so beseeching
I grasp how avoidance has wrought my course.

What She Gave Me

Their arrival forthright as a stopwatch
Every March slid inside my bachelor
Apartment's milk chute by whistling postmen
Boxes my mother winged over divides

Mountains would incline between us, candied
Peel and cherries drunk on brandy or rum
Eggs beaten in after siftings of flour
Baked, then swathed in bubble wrap and dispatched

Uniced, candles if unpacked set aflame
The years I'd blow out seldom passed alone
Consumed in thick slices before they went

Stale, my Murphy bed springing back unmade
Inside the wall on mornings stomached prone
The crumbs scattered from two plates not misspent.

Road Trip, Southern Alberta, 1986

West on Highway 5

For hours we rose through shelves of fenced-in land
The rusted curves of careless barbed wire pierced
From post to post between us and branded
Cattle browsing stubble, incurious

About what compelled us, subaqueous
Eyes dipped low as we breezed up right-angled
Roads, the grid shook ajar on unnoticed
Cordilleran lifts toward heights spangled

With snowfall and glaciers spread-eagled
In halting withdrawals true as your own
Erratic but sure, the divorce legal
Fateful roadmap unfolded years ago

The east lip of the lake about to curl
Before us: one shore grass, one mica-purled.

Approaching the u.s. Border, Waterton Lakes

Before us, one shore grass, one mica-purled
A cup of water tipped from zone to geo
Logic zone, the sky's affirming light dull
A ghost observed advancing tone by tone

Around us, taupe clouds sinking soft to hug
Close as we turned back from a floating line
Abstract between abutting countries, shrug
Of our tour boat putzing along benign

The acclaimed peaks we'd come to see obscure
Yet still you smiled, disappointment thwarted
By cleansing wind, no curtailed plan awkward
The water a neutral one-way mirror

Rocking your untroubled self on the move
Taxonomies of fish below absolved.

Estipah-skikikini-kots (Head-Smashed-In), Off Highway 785

Taxonomies of fish below absolved
Exact detail once would rout you always—
Or force your hand, impatience paraphrased
In how tersely you'd tidy and re-shelve

Clutter your children let drop, devolving
Into rising crises of plates left glazed
In sinks, dinner's traces erasing praise
You'd dismiss for having made it—no valve

Gave release—but here, looking down drive lanes
Where bison lost their footing, tumbled lame

In scores over this runnelled precipice
You stepped out of the car, pitched into awe
So steep a hungry calm let you ignore
Distant failures etched in faint hieroglyphs.

At an Early Age, Away from the Cities

Distant failures etched in faint hieroglyphs
Could you still see the son you'd trucked to Girl
Guide camp, a boy so small I was a doll
Your feral conscripts would have loved to dress

Badges racked up for *Loco-Parentis*
Spotters foiling my pratfalls into wells
At Sandy Lake, Mockingbird, or Tangle
Trees where, as mascot, I gorged on saskatoons

Too juiced on mauve to claim a gender yet
As I'd watch you every night lay a fire
Wash dishes in wild water you'd heated
The blackened stones encircling embers tiered

Under a metal bucket none upset
The flamed set of your eyes and lips inspired.

Áísínai'p (Writing-on-Stone), Off Highway 500

The flamed set of your eyes and lips inspired
By sunlit twists of gravelled roads beyond
The foothills in search of a missed, required

Exit, figments of dust raised in adorned
Coulees reaching fingers to the banks
Of the Milk, runoff's silt signatures signed

Below eroding sandstone bluffs rubbed smooth
By all they'd subsumed, pictographs not meant
For us: there to view, never to reprove

The man I'd turned into unexpected
A face you caught sight of, could not disprove
What you glimpsed gaining ground as more extant

Poise inscribed in the hoodoos' arabesques
Gestures humble despite what erasure risks.

Helicoptering to Mt. Assiniboine

Gestures humble despite what erasure risks
Who'd have guessed in years far ahead you'd want
Your eighth decade to clear approaching dusk
Where water parts from water, undaunted

By white noise overhead, rotors whisking
Us from the valley floor in angled feints
Deus ex Machina spiralled in brisk
Ellipses expanding, tightened to land

In the alpine, snowmelt's silence, as hoped
Astringent: scree and mountain columbine
The spellbound peak upended in the lake

Your reflection trickling down either slope's
Stark inclinations, nothing seen malign—
Your love, with little time to waste, unslaked.

Royal Stewart Dining Room, Prince of Wales Hotel, Waterton

Your love, with little time to waste, unslaked—
Separation, your obstacle and gift
Solitude unlooked-for, husband gone, opaque
Daughters storm-roused, wilful son raised on grit

You instilled, your drive accelerating
Past age beyond mountain gorges thrown wide
To rain-starved plains swept through unabated
The road paved, its vanishing point implied

Long before we'd chosen what to order
The meal's tablecloth an icefield, chilled wine
To quaff, Vivaldi's seasons embroidered
With change, the hired quartet's strings underlining

Variant spaces, what echoes span—
For hours we rose through shelves of fenced-in land.

Chosen Family

Crowd-Sickness

"This is what history looks like
and we must never forget it."
—JENNIFER WELSH

It's never felt as personal, and yet
Clicking through, we are ghosted by the noise

Of tides withdrawing, drowned bodies stetted
From what gets saved, but I see them still, boys

Overboard before the migrant boat sank
Their future, the BBC World Service

My DNA, my lost family tagged
On the genome, next to melting ice

Probes, launched from deserts, orbiting the sun
Drought flooding Syria with steady war

ABC reviving *American*
Idol, entrants streaming their hearts out, awed

Refugees aloof in Lebanese camps
Their feeds stuffed by Snapchat and Instagram.

After Rereading *A Stone Diary*

> "our eyes like
> the eyes of humans"
> —PAT LOWTHER

Displaced, they cross borders, the mountains cold
While men, while women leading their children
While children on their own, melt across them
Flow insistent, so quartz-brisk and molten—

Fled cities mortared—startled flood looking
Frozen, cracked seam of opal through feldspar
Glaciers, moonlit lamps sheathed by cirques far
Up, passes Europe strains to block they risk

Breaching to reach stoves with pots, beds with walls
Around them, windows they open, perhaps
Wash, not shelters but homes, the sky onyx
The stars pure in lands whose absolutes shall

Harbour them, though sometimes our dead are found
In rivers, weighted by stones or men's hands.

Utøya

How to swim past it, years after terror—
The island lodged in the brain's cold fjord
Remoteness of where her son died half-explored

Absences she makes herself face for raw
Glimpses of him, shards assembled before
The gunman fired: her boy, knelt among his

Murdered campmates, fearing what bullets risk
Ahead of the shockwaves mirrored ashore
What she hears, eyes closed, no storm can wash clean

Scarred beach glass the weightless surf obliges
To sing, glass humbled, tumbling glass in chime
Nerves jangling, lamentations night can't keep

To scale, her arms' impatient grasp of him
Losing muscle, his estrangement undimmed.

On Being Less

Those I set out with, they fade one by one
First fragments of sky, the cloudless mountains
An hour's drive from home, mauve fields of lupines
A foretaste of scree, the icebound glades stunned

By melt, sun a hatband of rising sweat
Three of us, then only two, my siblings
Burrs snarled in heavy winter fur, passing
Bighorn sheep moving higher to graze, crests

Shaggy with runoff, rambling torrents frayed
The windy highway west to weekend hikes
Leading to postcards displayed on my fridge

Camouflaging snapshots magnets array
Of self for self, of selves no longer like
The self I was, the wild unacknowledged.

A Longitudinal History of Solitude

Ogden Point Breakwater, Victoria

Ten-thousand, fifteen-ton blocks of granite

Quarried, cut, and barged from Hardy Island
Through the Inside Passage, as a helmet
Massed in nine immovable, unquestioned

Twenty-five-hundred-foot-long tiers over
A rock debris dredged nearby and dropped
To the seafloor, Babel's distraught tower

Pushed on its side, along which, above chop
Of tides, I reach its headstrong century-old
Occulting light flaring transcendence

Winked above the salt, silent self-control
Pulling free of undertow to amend
Interrupted thought, most ones and zeros

Washed clean of terabytes by spray's upthrow.

Tardy

"O my God, what am I
that these late mouths should cry open…"
—SYLVIA PLATH

This spring my season, the blooms so late they risk
Not blooming, so late it's fall, falling
Cherry petals a sheer psoriasis
Their translucence I brush off, mirror balls

Jostled by unruly, harried breezes
Fuzzy dice swinging in the sky's windshield
Each one untangling, circus floss yielding
Stillness, Zen's pink, branching solar systems raised

And ravaged, their satori telescoped
One day starkly rose, salmon-dull the next
Flesh flayed from thinning bones as we spawn

Petals eyes staring up from myopic
Pools of rain, awareness precarious
Eros a bough naked against the dawn.

Oxygen

We were close. My iPhone scrolling us through

Photos I took to show you, a last glimpse
In your final days, though we had no clue
Or would not see or must have looked askance.

I did, at least. In your hospital room
Chair drawn up to your bed. Oxygen tank
Hung overhead, not unlike a vacuum

Cleaner canister, you breathing in banks
Of purifying air; cheerful, loving
While affirming the flora you knew well

Camas, grape hyacinth, dogwood, quince—spring
Weeks old, as if its efflorescent spell
When stemmed, could carry forward still; grateful

For your poised life with us; as I'm grateful.

Hive Mind

after Robert Mapplethorpe's *Flowers*

I take closeups of flowers not shots of men
Who walk by me, a stung apiarist

Not lily-livered, the blooms tacitly
Within reach, unlike men whose thirsts I'd tend

The turned loam I would lay them down in moist
And blossom-splattered, big-globed dahlias

In curbside beds an incunabula
Of jutting anthers, men loved in the past

Retouched, resolutely re-engineered
Sans shadow, lighting aboveboard, knob-kneed

Stems and gaunt-chested leaves made to swivel
In contrapposto, hips and canted rears

Imposing when swung, shook petals seeming
To part, salute my aloof appraisal.

To part, salute my aloof appraisal
To dissemble my focus, bees amass

Somersault into saxifrage from phlox—
Hived psyches abuzz, bodies espousal

Gauzy trumpets savaged, nuzzled by stings
My response to love anaphylactic

A swelling some call a lapsing sceptic's
Ecstasy, my stem unstemmed before zing

Michelangelo's butt-plugging *David*
With mock orange, his pale rose roseate

Pierced marble body and deviant mind
Derangements panoramic, dazzled beds

Of asters my cosmos, what inchoate
Shooting stars cometing past to blind me.

Shooting stars cometing past to blind me
I place an ad: "calla lily looking

For same," my spadix a distended hook
Shrouded inside a tight spathe, spellbinding

Only after it's posted and swiped through
Skipped over because one of too many

Too alike, hoods flaring white and creamy
The stems, when cut, lazily thrown askew

In vases where slim pickings ache to share
Domestic leanings, bonds thorny to shoot

On glass-top tables what's limply wanted—
Turn up the lights, flesh out partial truths bared

In bytes with real blooms, desire re-rooted
Water-lust half-lived but consummated.

Water-lust half-lived but consummated
Despoiled blooms tossed aside starting to wilt

Bees whizzing by, pollens they'd gathered spilt
Hairy legs bearing no trace, not soulmates

Privy to lootings dreamt slow but rapid
Beauty disposed to last until it can

No more, flown as fast as a courtesan
Whose dropped petals leave him shy when naked

Eternity over, the life cycle
From bulb to bloom a splashy recurrence

Each bud goes through once only, its moment
To explode open pyrotechnical

Then, fast past prime, it droops to prurience—
My floral voyeurism expedient.

My floral voyeurism expedient—
Each dewy nosegay virtue-signalling

A love for display, little else channelled
Ardour whetted for summer's abundant

Supply of gladioli to arrange
In crystal, swords in tiers radiating

Outwards and upwards to accentuate
Stature and girth, damp splendour unchanging

Unless those rapiers vanish from stores
My virtue sapped of sharpened outlet

And I find myself trolling for pictures
The picked-over nursery sites adored

For their blunt candour, parched showy coquettes
In facsimile, not real but richer.

In facsimile, not real but richer
Ceci n'est pas une fleur, some artist said

A man is not a man unless in bed
Soil mulched and roots dowsed under copper beech

Branches outspread overhead to provide
A break from sun, humusy counterpane

Raked smooth to his chin or pulling away
Nipple bared, ground next to him unoccupied

The posies I'd posted taken offline
The earth fallow, nitrogen water's drained

From my anthered allotment given time
To refresh: little deaths, seeds I've denied

This garden running wild mine to sustain
Those few perennials I sow sublime.

Those few perennials I sow sublime
A field for bees whose growth I leave uncut

Men I've loved till now a compatriot
Monoculture honeycombed with ill-timed

Dry seasons, the hives close to dying out
Remorse a pollen no one can harvest

Longing making me sneeze, nose pointillist
In its nascent acuity, each bout

Of loss forcing me to feel less and less
Immune to droning on alone, annuals

Serial monogamists frost constrains
What I've started planting low maintenance

But flamboyant while, setting down my trowel
I take closeups of flowers not shots of men.

Last of the Catchers

I've never caught sight of what they catch, boys
Static as old men, old men less awkward

Than boys, patient as herons, as lizards
Wrists flicked quick as tongues, flies pierced and deployed

The lines cast far and teased, cast far and teased
What cold voids the hooks slip through, flat and clear

As quartz, or rough, catchers swamped as waves rear
The lines cast far and teased, cast far and teased

Neither sculpin nor octopi striking
On bait, stone blocks stood on descending stairs

Numb to the logic they ballast below
Insistent tides as the cormorants shriek

Torpedo through reflected sky to spear
Vanished prey, shrugging off the undertow.

Emily Carr, Synecdoche

Stories read aloud haunt me still, a voice
Steeped in salmon and cedar, the steamer
She sailed between islands reinforced
By mosquitoes, rain, and mist, eyes streaming

My mother, pages opened in her lap
Straight-backed chair drawn to my bed, alive
When she was alive, routes they travelled shaped
By what none could say or think, but contrived

As elegy, sloped poles not abandoned
But seized, the carvers not gone but made sick
By how bark was stripped, the tools forbidden
To give trees rightful form, heartwood quickened

By proxies, how her pictures make its grain
What we know: wet, socked-in coast adzed of names.

Míqən

Sheltered behind a screen of wind-ravished
Arbutus, their roots picked out in camas
And fawn lilies outrun by narcissus
I've scaled the slope they rise above, burnished

By salt lifting from the sea, those who first
Lay against it to sky-gaze unrehearsed
In views the next to come had transplanted
A tipped savanna of traits, cloudy slant

Imposed on what's lasted as knowable
But private about Earth, our scavenging
Aloof idiolect eroding range
Anyone this climb rakes susceptible

To what the land's inclined to speak, this hill
Warmed by the sun, my face heat-washed as till.

Under the Rainbow

The breakwater reaches its placid branch

Through the haze, the mitred joints aiming me
Right slightly and slightly right again, wrenched

Granite blocks loosened by the waves' freefall
Chaos, automated beacon flashing
Access, mute wind calm, sun refracting

Overhead, bands of light: intractable
Fan blades shaken open, each airy wash

Of washed-in colour untold fathoms wide
A short-lived pergola to stand beneath
A memorial arch, its ribs corsaged

With drizzle, my limbs re-limned as warmth slides
Downwards, icy mangle ironing sheets

Petal-thin, wrinkles steaming till they're gone.

Awareness While Shaving

The face, how long can I face it, give it
A chin, nose sloped below skewed eyes, stubbly
Hang-dog cheeks set loose before they bracket
A flatlining mouth, a not-untroubled

Conjuror's trick dropped in place when I turn
Impassive from the mirror, an unrouged scrim
Against which ambition plays, my lines learned
By rote, gouged in deep, undermined by whims

Pure *commedia dell'arte*, sad yet
Not falsely happy, the shore in between
Razored where tides draw a line, abetted
By retreating sharpness, the brackish keen

Edge of it making less porous my skin
A screen door to peer out as well as in.

An Epistemology

> "why tell me then
> there is something wrong with my eyes"
> —MARGARET ATWOOD

The world when viewed clearly, the poet says
Is viewed through tears, but my eyes long bloodshot
Have dried, are lucid or glassy, will not
Look, or look away, what's seen not erased

By being glanced at or turned away from
Plain sight making what is glimpsed proximate
Or distant, love and hate two intimates
Chance accommodates, each of which amend

What my bathroom mirror frames while I shave
A life sentence of mirrors in time lapse
The years a flipbook of self-portraits grasped
Or left dog-eared, sped-up moral sense graved

In my eyes, the world slowed down by gazing
Inward, caring realized through reflecting.

Chosen Family

Coasting above the sun-drenched sequoias
Anchored in your backyard, wingtips touching

Shadows turning—skydivers with hands joined
Who've yet to come to ground—the thermals quaffed

Pouring them through ellipses, tipped spirals
Uncoiled and rewound, feathers wind-tethered

Kaleidoscopic when light-struck, a braille
The eye runs across, the air read lower

Down where we sit brimming, gazing up thrilled
Your table holding us to a circle

Buoyant with cheeses and glasses of chilled
Tequila, words unplanned, luffed vertical—

A prayer held in beaks of like-minded steel
The Earth spinning, four eagles a sun wheel.

Heirloom, Opening The Circle

Your maternal grandfather's gold bracelet
Giving weight to my wrist, hammered tongue loosed
From the clasp after he died, a surfeit
Of uncoiling ancestral links abstruse

When not worn, what they forge—patient helix
Time passes on—a bond made clear, of care
Each generation encircles the next
With, and the next, unknowing but aware

The man he was you would never meet, gone
The year you were born—ghostly talisman
Catching and keeping track of the eye, shone
By all you were told of him and now hand

On to me, light looping from me to him
Codifying my wrist, his metonym.

Feng Shui Unbound

You longed for a wingback chair and window
Never found the ideal matching pair
Countless arms too low, seats soft, slanted glare
Double panes of glass slid across your floor

Outlining the slim-fitting solitude
You kept on wearing, knot in your single
Necktie rubbing silk to naught, prodigal
In all but time, the gauzy interlude

We would call our youth fading back toward
Upholstered layers of dusk, men you'd looked for
In sunless bars leading to candlelit

Meals served to old friends, laid-in wines uncorked ·
At the large makeshift table you adore
Straight-back chairs pulled in close a squaring fit.

Inside the Frame

Kept to one floor, he rolls his chair from bed
To easel, weekdays spent behind windows
Houseflies walk across, the light-torn, rain-bled
Squares of glass they lift from, blankly going

Where he cannot, grandchildren in and out
Wife opening her florist's shop, daughter
Attentive, busy, wheeling him around
Time an island trapped by shallow water

He paints his mornings out of, each canvas
A sail catching what flails inside a frame
He turns windward to make bell out, nexus
Of what could albatross the picture plane

Unbound by able brushstrokes, an old man's
Youthful sightlines stretched life-sized, a life's span.

Three Amazing Things I Saw On Thursday

"Life remains a blessing
Although you cannot bless."
—W. H. AUDEN

While I was out walking late one evening

Toward the Salish Sea beneath dusk-stained
Chestnuts, the lanterns' budding flames sustained

By rain-rinsed air, the calm unplumbed meaning

Behind the peacocks' crazed, sitar-sharp cries
Unscored, I stopped to watch a freshly horned

Stag twist blossoms off bent-low and forlorn
Boughs of cherry, his soft lips grimaced wide

The tide laid flat on the bias as blue

Milky linen to the shore where I next
Stood, waves rucked against the dimness stars shed

A single dangling thread of mist slipped through
A gap in the Sooke Hills until the last

Of tangential day was, by crispness, spread.

Photo Finish

Photo Finish

If I'm conscious when it comes, I am sure
I won't notice the stills I have squandered
Wink out: one instant, sun's photogravure
Catching me unaware, wrapped in laundered

Cotton, awake but damp in my mother's
Short-lived arms; the next, I locate myself
Levelled onto settled pillows, splinters
Of half-light eyelashed by louvred blinds, sylphs

Of ebbing haze last to wander across
Threadbare retina before I realize
I've nothing left to see, a spun-out dross
Of tone so filtered I am tranquillized

Awarded interrupted sight, my long
Grey eyes filmy, at one time celadon.

Grey eyes filmy, at one time celadon
I'd roll them skyward, gaze up, unseeing
Childish worldview not mapping much beyond
What it began with: seeing hinged scalene

Eyeballs wandering, slant-rhyming movers
Out of plumb, since birth at cross-purposes
A pooled lack of shared focus making swerve
What unities they saw, thought's bypasses

Halving, before seen to, hearts into ears
Crosses doubled into telegraph poles
Ether counted backwards through, love a slur
Till socketed muscles woke in control

Turn-range reined in by suture, enabled
The Brownie I shortly held more stable.

The Brownie I shortly held more stable
As it snapped the snubbed rubbish of boyhood
With photo corners what's unplaceable
Hung against velvety black paper should

I have then wanted to, tongue dim with glue
Bleached-out foretastes of monotone parents
And pets (age, sequence, and names hitherto
Gone missing): iguanas, kittens, parrots

Dogs collaged in multiple exposures
Their restlessness, shade by frozen shade, best
Unleashed once the gated albums are closed
The self not in the instances saved, lost

If leafed through, pages browsed never equal
To what I lived, vignette without sequel.

To what I lived, vignette without sequel
I brought a stuck turning away from death
Disbelief in nonbeing habitual
The photos' trimmed white borders adding depth

To greyscale, my doubtful Instamatic
Aimed away from myself, the rolls of film
Unbiased, their conscience automatic
Suggestible, a slippery medium

To rewind and develop, negatives
Slid into Glassine sleeves before the prints
Go astray, the mind's offhand eye furtive
Witness to what I looked for while squinting

Into too much light, each male friend I took
A shadow outlined by the sun, face blank.

A shadow outlined by the sun, face blank
I let my skin brown, compassing little
Of love, my lens autofocus, lanky
Amusements romantic but rote, blissful

Crises unspooled along solitary
Beach roads, absent a map to sight the heart—
Maze without still point or exit, entry
A sheltered bay, drive guarded from the start—

Photos of men I would find not taken
Profusely, trips to earthquake zones due south
Barely talked of after, pink sand shaken
From shorts and T-shirts packed unwashed, my mouth

Rimed with grit, illusions twenty-twenty
For a few years still, hopeful of plenty.

For a few years, still hopeful of plenty
I escaped wearing progressives, my eyes
Assessed to see what's surely there clearly
Enough to seem perceptive and deny

The body's stalled, time-lapsed weakness for change
What quotidian I've left fixed to be
Flawless, inconceivably within range
Of the real, a focused maturity

Rogue existence never failed to make blur
The flesh ageing absurdly, counterpoint
To all I'd aspired to, desire's flâneur
The labyrinth I walked inconsequent

No blind spots lit at its unsightly core
Solitude my bedmate and minotaur.

Solitude my bedmate and minotaur
The sleep ahead, although fine it may be
It's no less private, a rumpled eyesore
No one wakes us from, my apartment clean

Less abyss than a set where I enact
My purpose, corners and turns in the hall
Scaring up points of view so inexact
I embody them best when alone, small

Livestreamed outtakes, each correction a short
Disclosure but, if spliced, they make a life
Long—over fast but eternal—import
Shadowy till rendered still more aloof

By death, the timing a kindness I shall endure
If I am conscious when it comes, I am sure.

ACKNOWLEDGEMENTS

I would like to thank the editors and staff of the following literary journals for their interest and for choosing the poems that they published: *Alberta Views* ("Kananaskis Country"), *Arc* ("A Twentieth-Century Roadmap to Settler Architecture"), *Canadian Literature* ("What We Live For"), *Event* ("After Rereading *A Stone Diary*," "Utøya"), *The Fiddlehead* ("Bathhouse Raids, Toronto, 1981," "Bombardment, September 1940," "Coda for the Victims," "Folded on the Steps of the Museum of Broken Relationships," "HIV: A History," "Misophonia"), *Gay and Lesbian Review Worldwide* ("Late Show, Minneapolis, 1977"), *Literary Review of Canada* ("*Malus Pumila*"), *The Malahat Review* ("For David Wojnarowicz," "Kenny's Bracelet"), *The Maynard* ("Tchaikovsky, Age 52, Finds His Inspiration"), *Ottawater* ("*Blessed Are*," "Rock Hudson, Safer Sex, and What Comes Next"), *Riddle Fence* ("Arrival and Departure," "Butterflies Are Free," "Call from the Top," "In Memory of Your Thirteenth Birthday"), *The Road Not Taken* ("Melittology"), *Speckled Trout Review* ("Ardingly"), *Storm Cellar* ("They Always Get Their Man"), *Vallum* ("A Google Maps View of the House Where I Grew Up," "Last of the Catchers"), and *The Walrus* ("School of Xerez Fino").

Poems also originally appeared or were republished in the following anthologies and chapbooks: "Feng Shui Unbound" in *Thirteen* (Toronto: League of Canadian Poets, 2019), "Misophonia" in *Windsock* (Victoria: Frog Hollow, 2018), "Pop Music Stigmata" in *Voicing Suicide* (Victoria: Ekstasis, 2020), and "A Son's Nineteen Seventies Wardrobe" in *Hologram for PK Page* (Victoria: Ekstasis, 2021).

Thanks is due to the Canada Council for the Arts for its support in 2018 and 2019, underwriting the composition of 366 sonnets in total, of which *Lost Family* is a generous sample.

I am indebted to Molly Peacock who, during a visit to the University of Victoria that I had arranged while I was the editor of *The Malahat Review*, enamoured me of the sonnet. I accompanied Molly on a visit to Carla Funk's poetry workshop in the Department of Writing, where she explained the virtues of the form to unsuspecting second-year students—and to me. In order to participate in the thirty-minute writing session that followed Molly's detailing of the rules (during which she compared writing fourteen lines to the progressively smooth unrolling of a yoga mat), I had to borrow a pen from the young poet on my left. After sketching out a complete first draft of my first sonnet (uncollected here) within the prescribed time, I was hooked. As Don Paterson says in the introduction to *101 Sonnets from Shakespeare to Heaney* (London: Faber, 1999), "Sonnets make it easy for poets to write poems." Writing good ones is another matter.

Many friends supported me while I wrote many of these sonnets, including Joe Bishop, Yvonne Blomer, Ali Blythe, Eric Folsom, Alisa Gordaneer, Anita Lahey, Ben Ladouceur, Ross Leckie, Scott Lemoine, Ian LeTourneau, Elizabeth-Anne Malischewski, Shane Neilson, Arleen Paré, Caryl Peters, Philip Robert, Bill Ralston, Doug Schmidt, and Derk and Eva Wynand. In particular, I would like to thank Kyeren Regehr, who, on the countless occasions that we met for coffee and to exchange poems, eagerly asked me to read her more sonnets, thereby keeping me equally engaged, as if I were writing a novel in serial form for an avid, capacious readership. Everyone at Véhicule Press has been so wonderfully supportive of my intentions in this book, including Simon Dardick, Jennifer Varkonyi, Willow Little, and David Drummond, whose wonderful cover design is its perfect calling card. I would especially also like to thank Carmine Starnino, my editor at Signal Editions, who affirmed the merit of my approach to sonnet-writing and took to *Lost Family* practically on faith.

In order of appearance, the epigraphs are from: Ethan Mordden, *How's Your Romance* (New York: St. Martin's, 2005); Henry Green, *Caught* (New York: NYRB, [1943] 2016); James Baldwin, *Giovanni's Room*. New York: Dell, [1956]1988); Roland Barthes, "Preface," in Renaud Camus, *Tricks: Twenty-Five Encounters*, translated by Richard Howard (New York; London: High Risk, [1981] 1996); Chris Lowe, Neil Tennant, and Allee Willis, "What have I done to deserve this" (Cage Music/10 Music/MCA Music, 1987); David B. Feinberg, *Eighty-Sixed* (New York: Viking, 1989); W. H. Auden, "September 1, 1939" in *Collected Poems* (New York: Vintage, 1979); William Blake, "The Tyger" in *Collected Poems* (New York: Routledge, 2002); Jennifer Welsh, *The Return of History* (Toronto: Anansi, 2016); Pat Lowther, "In the Silence Between" in *A Stone Diary* (Toronto: Oxford, 1977); Sylvia Plath, "Poppies in October" in *Ariel* (London: Faber, 1965); Margaret Atwood, "Notes Towards a Poem That Can Never Be Written" in *True Stories* (Toronto: Oxford, 1981), and W. H. Auden, "As I walked out one evening" in *Collected Poems* (New York: Vintage, 1979). The last line of "Pop Music Stigmata" is from "Do You Believe," a song by Melanie on *Stoneground Words* (Neighborhood Records, 1972). The first line of "A Son's Nineteen-Seventies Wardrobe" is from "Arras" by P. K. Page from *The Essential P. K. Page*, edited by Arlene Lampert and Théa Gray (Erin: The Porcupine's Quill, 2008).

Garry Neill Kennedy's *My Fourth Grade Class*, which inspired "Who, Where, Why, When," is held in the collection of the National Gallery of Canada in Ottawa. "Ganymede's Coeval" retells the story behind "Six Letters in Autumn and One Unwritten," a poem from my book, *Notes Toward A Family Tree* (Kingston: Quarry, 1993). "Zipless fuck," which I use in "After Rereading *Eighty-Sixed*" and which David B. Feinberg also references in his novel, was coined by Erica Jong in *Fear of Flying* (New York: Holt, Rinehart and Winston, 1973). GMHC in "Age of Foolish Risk" stands for Gay Men's Health Crisis, a still-extant New York-based AIDS-support organization founded in 1982 during the early days of the pandemic. I first encountered the title of "Crowd Sickness," as a term to describe the chronic ill effects of Internet overstimulation, in Michael Harris' *Solitude: In Pursuit of a Singular Life in a Crowded World* (Toronto: Doubleday, 2017). The title of "Míqən," which is pronounced "MEE-gan" and means "warmed by the sun," describes the slope down to the ocean from the Lookout in Victoria's Beacon Hill Park; it is from Lekwungen, a dialect of North Straits Salish, the language spoken by the Lekwungen, the original inhabitants of the unceded lands upon which the city and its diverse inhabitants from around the world, including me, gratefully reside.

The following poems are dedicated to: "Tchaikovsky, Age 52, Finds His Inspiration" (Kyeren Regehr), "The Love Song of Dusty Springfield" (Bill Ralston), "Folded on the Steps of the Museum of Broken Relationships" (Elizabeth-Anne Malischewski and Robert Sweeny), "Kenny's Bracelet" (Magie Dominic), "My Epistemology" (Jan Zwicky), and "Feng Shui Unbound" (Philip Robert). "Chosen Family" and "Heirloom, Opening the Circle" are dedicated to the memory of Eva Wynand and to her husband, Derk Wynand; "Family Epidemic" and "Oxygen" to the memory of my aunt, Barbara Preston, and also in memory of my uncle, John Preston; "Bombardment, September 1940, to the memory of my paternal grandmother, Mary Barton; "In a West Coast Garden" to the memory of my maternal grandmother, Margaret Preston; "A Retrospective" to the memory of my godmother, Margaret Young; "Gefilte Fish" to the memory of Lala Heine Koehn; and "Inside the Frame" to the memory of James Gordaneer and also to his family. As well as to my sister, Pam Barton, *Lost Family* is dedicated to her husband, Doug James, to the memory of my parents, Nancy Barton and Richard Barton, and to my one surviving sister, Sue Schroder.

ALSO BY JOHN BARTON

POETRY

A Poor Photographer
Hidden Structure
West of Darkness: Emily Carr, a Self-Portrait
Great Men
Notes Toward a Family Tree
Designs from the Interior
Sweet Ellipsis
Hypothesis
Hymn
For the Boy with the Eyes of the Virgin: Selected Poems
Polari

ESSAYS

We Are Not Avatars: Essays, Memoirs, Manifestos

CHAPBOOKS

Destinations, Leaving the Map
Oxygen
Shroud
Runoff
Asymmetries (In the House of the Present and The Strata)
Balletomane: The Program Notes of Lincoln Kirsten
Reframing Paul Cadmus
Visible Not Seen: Queer Expression in the Age of Equity
Windsock

EDITOR

Silences
belles lettres / beautiful letters

We All Begin in a Little Magazine: Arc and the Promise
of Canada's Poets, 1978–1998
Seminal: The Anthology of Canada's Gay Male Poets
The Malahat Review at Fifty: Canada's Iconic Literary Journal
The Essential Douglas LePan
The Essential Derk Wynand

IN TRANSLATION
À l'ouest de l'ombre. Emily Carr, un auto-portrait

INDEX OF TITLES

Signal
EDITIONS

Carmine Starnino, Editor
Michael Harris, Founding Editor

MAPPING THE CHAOS Rhea Tregebov
FIRE NEVER SLEEPS Carla Hartsfield
THE RHINO GATE POEMS George Ellenbogen
SHADOW CABINET Richard Sanger
MAP OF DREAMS Ricardo Sternberg
THE NEW WORLD Carmine Starnino
THE LONG COLD GREEN EVENINGS OF SPRING Elisabeth Harvor
KEEP IT ALL Yves Boisvert (Translated by Judith Cowan)
THE GREEN ALEMBIC Louise Fabiani
THE ISLAND IN WINTER Terence Young
A TINKERS' PICNIC Peter Richardson
SARACEN ISLAND: THE POEMS OF ANDREAS KARAVIS David Solway
BEAUTIES ON MAD RIVER: SELECTED AND NEW POEMS Jan Conn
WIND AND ROOT Brent MacLaine
HISTORIES Andrew Steinmetz
ARABY Eric Ormsby
WORDS THAT WALK IN THE NIGHT Pierre Morency
    (Translated by Lissa Cowan and René Brisebois)
A PICNIC ON ICE: SELECTED POEMS Matthew Sweeney
HELIX: NEW AND SELECTED POEMS John Steffler
HERESIES: THE COMPLETE POEMS OF ANNE WILKINSON, 1924-1961
    Edited by Dean Irvine
CALLING HOME Richard Sanger
FIELDER'S CHOICE Elise Partridge
MERRYBEGOT Mary Dalton
MOUNTAIN TEA Peter Van Toorn
AN ABC OF BELLY WORK Peter Richardson
RUNNING IN PROSPECT CEMETERY Susan Glickman
MIRABEL Pierre Nepveu (Translated by Judith Cowan)
POSTSCRIPT Geoffrey Cook
STANDING WAVE Robert Allen
THERE, THERE Patrick Warner
HOW WE ALL SWIFTLY: THE FIRST SIX BOOKS Don Coles
THE NEW CANON: AN ANTHOLOGY OF CANADIAN POETRY
    Edited by Carmine Starnino
OUT TO DRY IN CAPE BRETON Anita Lahey
RED LEDGER Mary Dalton
REACHING FOR CLEAR David Solway
OX Christopher Patton
THE MECHANICAL BIRD Asa Boxer
SYMPATHY FOR THE COURIERS Peter Richardson
MORNING GOTHIC: NEW AND SELECTED POEMS George Ellenbogen
36 CORNELIAN AVENUE Christopher Wiseman
THE EMPIRE'S MISSING LINKS Walid Bitar
PENNY DREADFUL Shannon Stewart
THE STREAM EXPOSED WITH ALL ITS STONES D.G. Jones
PURE PRODUCT Jason Guriel
ANIMALS OF MY OWN KIND Harry Thurston
BOXING THE COMPASS Richard Greene
CIRCUS Michael Harris

Véhicule Press